Sacagawea

Brave Explorer

by Jodie Shepherd

Content Consultant
Nanci R. Vargus, Ed.D.
Professor Emeritus, University of Indianapolis

Reading Consultant
Jeanne M. Clidas, Ph.D.
Reading Specialist

Children's Press®
An Imprint of Scholastic Inc.

Library of Congress Cataloging-in-Publication Data
Shepherd, Jodie.
  Sacagawea / by Jodie Shepherd.
    pages cm. -- (Rookie biographies)
  Includes index.
  ISBN 978-0-531-21414-5 (library binding) -- ISBN 978-0-531-21427-5 (pbk.)
  1. Sacagawea--Juvenile literature. 2. Shoshoni women--Biography--Juvenile
literature. 3. Shoshoni Indians--Biography--Juvenile literature. 4. Lewis and Clark
Expedition (1804-1806)--Juvenile literature. I. Title.

  F592.7.S123S54 2015
  978.0049745740092--dc23
  [B]   2015017321

Produced by Spooky Cheetah Press
Design by Keith Plechaty

© 2016 by Scholastic Inc.

All rights reserved. Published in 2016 by Children's Press, an imprint of Scholastic Inc.

Printed in China 62

SCHOLASTIC, CHILDREN'S PRESS, ROOKIE BIOGRAPHIES®, and associated logos
are trademarks and/or registered trademarks of Scholastic Inc.

1 2 3 4 5 6 7 8 9 10 R 25 24 23 22 21 20 19 18 17 16

Photographs ©: cover: Robert Schoeller; 3 top left: Vladimir Wrangel/Shutterstock,
Inc.; 3 top right: Mike Theiler/Getty Images; 3 bottom: North Wind Picture Archives;
4: Michael Haynes, www.mhaynesart.com; 7: W.H. Jackson/The New York Historical
Society/Getty Images; 11: Washington State Historical Society/Art Resource, NY; 12:
MPI/Getty Images; 15 top: Fotosearch/Getty Images; 15 bottom: National Historical
Park, Independence, Missouri, MO, USA/Bridgeman Images; 16: Ed Vebell/Getty
Images; 19: Washington State Historical Society/Art Resource, NY; 20: Washington
State Historical Society/Art Resource, NY; 23: North Wind Picture Archives; 24: Wood
Ronsaville Harlin, Inc. USA/Bridgeman Images; 28: Franz-Marc Frei/Corbis Images;
30 top left: Michael Haynes, www.mhaynesart.com; 30 top right: Mike Theiler/Getty
Images; 31 top: Washington State Historical Society/Art Resource, NY; 31 center: Ed
Vebell/Getty Images; 31 bottom: Washington State Historical Society/Art Resource, NY.

Maps by XNR Productions, Inc.

Table of Contents

4

Meet Sacagawea

In 1805, a young American Indian woman led a team of **explorers**. They went across thousands of miles of wilderness. Sacagawea (Sa-cah-GUH-we-ah) guided them along mountains and rivers. She helped them deal peacefully with the different people they met. And she did it all while carrying her baby on her back!

No one knows Sacagawea's exact birth date. She was born sometime between 1788 and 1790. She lived in an area that is now part of the state of Idaho. Sacagawea was a member of the Shoshone (shuh-SHOW-nee) tribe. She lived with her parents, two brothers, and a sister.

The Shoshones were wanderers. They moved from place to place, carrying their teepees with them. They hunted, fished, and gathered berries and roots.

This photo shows a Shoshone village.

teepee

7

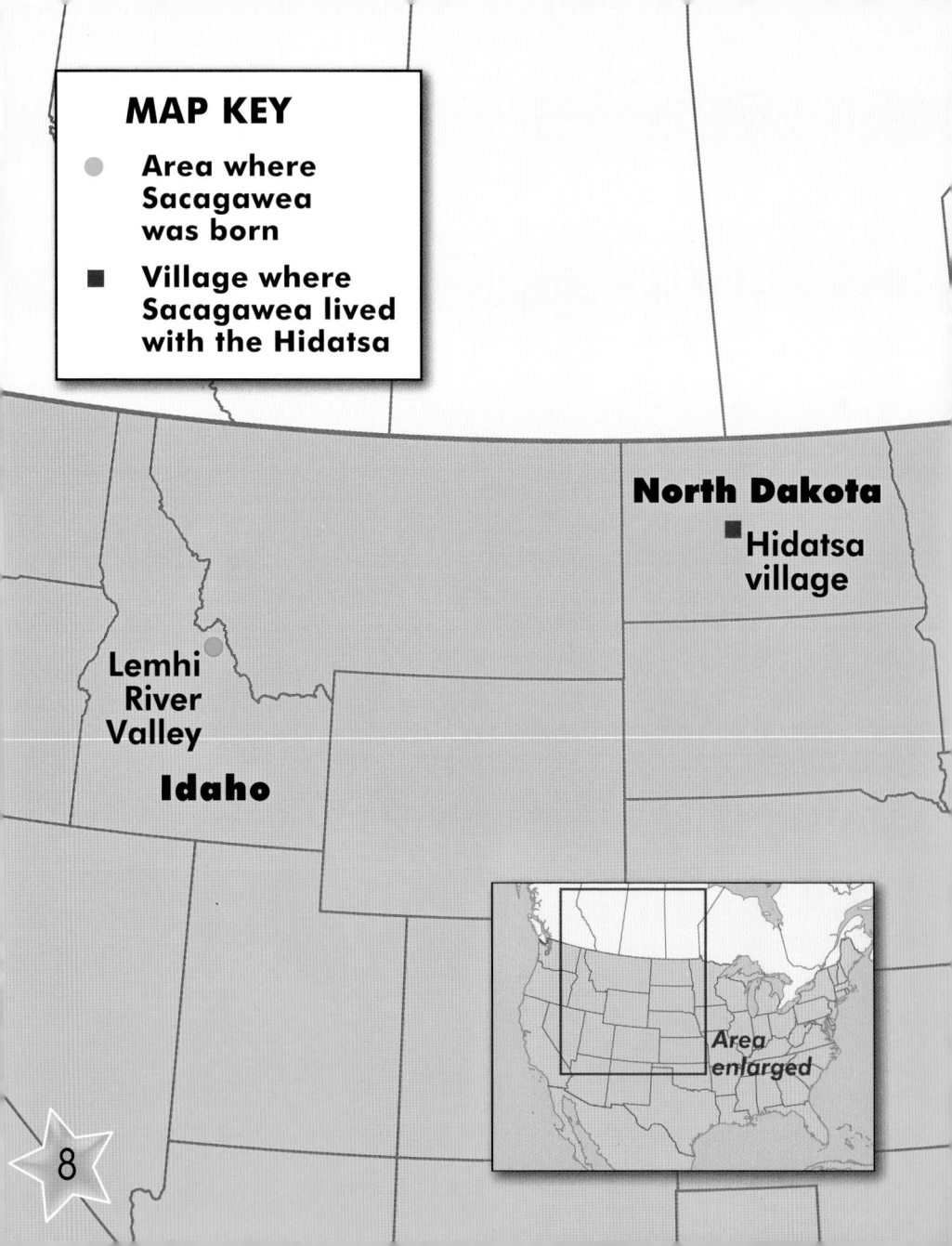

MAP KEY

- Area where Sacagawea was born
- Village where Sacagawea lived with the Hidatsa

North Dakota
- Hidatsa village

Lemhi River Valley

Idaho

Area enlarged

When Sacagawea was 10 or 11 years old, she was captured by Hidatsa (hee-DAHT-suh) Indians. They took her back to their own village. Her life changed completely. She began to speak Hidatsa. She learned to grow crops.

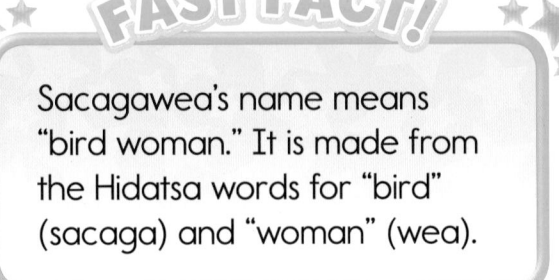

FAST FACT!

Sacagawea's name means "bird woman." It is made from the Hidatsa words for "bird" (sacaga) and "woman" (wea).

When she was 15 years old, Sacagawea married a fur trapper named Toussaint (TOO-sahn) Charbonneau (SHAR-buh-noh). Later, they had a baby boy together. Before long, this little family would start on a big adventure.

Charbonneau

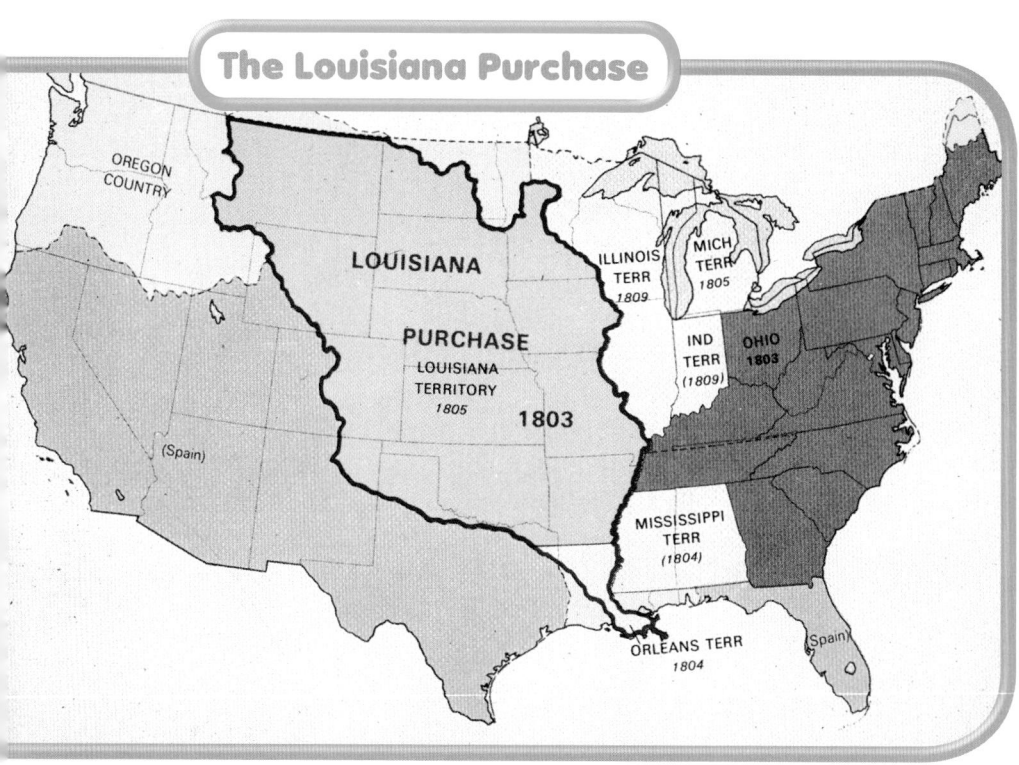

The Louisiana Purchase

OREGON COUNTRY

LOUISIANA

PURCHASE

LOUISIANA TERRITORY 1805

1803

(Spain)

ILLINOIS TERR 1809

MICH TERR 1805

IND TERR (1809)

OHIO 1803

MISSISSIPPI TERR (1804)

ORLEANS TERR 1804

(Spain)

This map shows the land gained through the Louisiana Purchase. Most of the land to the right of that area (dark orange and light blue) already belonged to the United States. The land to the left belonged to other countries.

The Louisiana Purchase

The United States was still a new country in 1803. It was much smaller than it is today. President Thomas Jefferson believed the country should grow. So he bought a big piece of land from France. That sale was called the Louisiana Purchase. It doubled the size of the United States.

President Jefferson wanted to learn more about this new land. He chose his secretary Meriwether Lewis to head an **expedition**. Lewis asked his friend William Clark to help him lead the group of explorers.

FAST FACT!

Lewis and Clark led a group of more than 30 explorers. They called themselves the Corps (KOR) of Discovery.

Captain Meriwether Lewis

Captain William Clark

15

Lewis and Clark had a big job to do. They would try to find a river **route** that led to the Pacific Ocean. They would also study the people, plants, and animals they saw along the way. Finally, they would draw maps of the land as they passed through. But who could guide them through the wild country?

This painting shows the Corps of Discovery sailing on the Missouri River.

Sacagawea Sets Out

Lewis and Clark met Sacagawea when they reached North Dakota in 1804. She spoke two American Indian languages. She had lived out west and knew the land. Sacagawea was just the person to guide the expedition.

FAST FACT!

Sacagawea's young baby, Jean-Baptiste, went on the trip! Clark nicknamed him "Pomp."

20

The explorers headed west on April 7, 1805. Sacagawea helped guide the group. She **interpreted** American Indian languages. She helped set up camp and found roots and plants to eat. She also sewed and repaired clothing. Baby Pomp rode in a cradleboard strapped to his mother's back.

Sacagawea helped the explorers talk to people they met.

Sacagawea could be counted on in an emergency, too. One day, as the group sailed along the Missouri River, one of the boats began to fill with water. Some supplies and papers began to float away. Charbonneau froze in fear. But Sacagawea stayed calm. She rescued almost everything.

This is one of the journals
from the expedition.

The group finally arrived at a place Sacagawea knew well. It was her childhood home. She was excited to see her old Shoshone friends. Even more exciting: Sacagawea's brother was now the chief of the tribe!

Sacagawea convinced her brother to help the explorers. He gave them horses to carry them through the Rocky Mountains. He sent Shoshone guides to help show them the way.

End of the Adventure

In November 1805, Sacagawea and the explorers finally reached the Pacific Ocean. They had traveled more than 4,000 miles (6,437 kilometers). And they were only half finished! They still had to make the long trip home.

FAST FACT!

In 2000, the U.S. government honored Sacagawea. They made a one-dollar coin that shows her with baby Pomp strapped to her back.

The Lewis and Clark Expedition

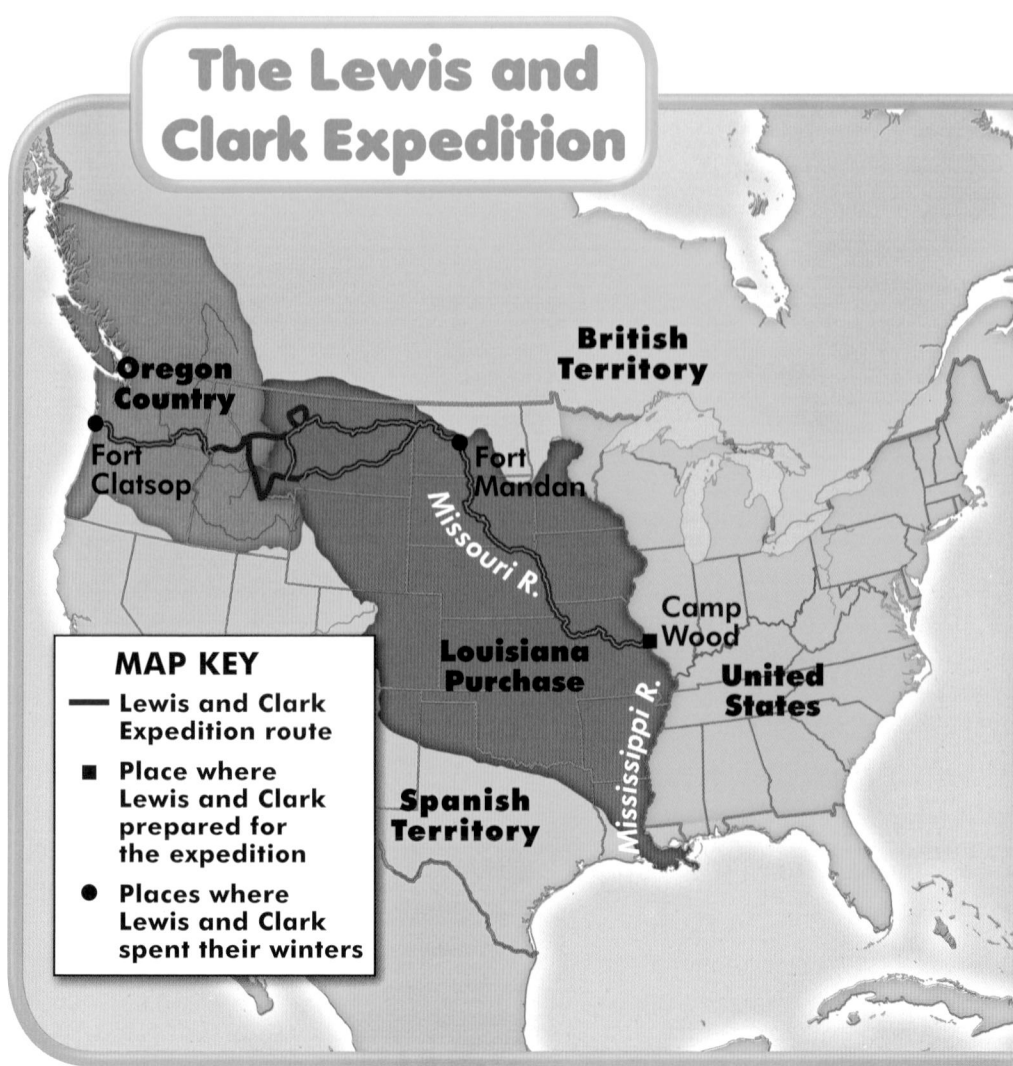

Oregon Country

Fort Clatsop

British Territory

Fort Mandan

Missouri R.

Louisiana Purchase

Camp Wood

Mississippi R.

United States

Spanish Territory

MAP KEY

— Lewis and Clark Expedition route

■ Place where Lewis and Clark prepared for the expedition

● Places where Lewis and Clark spent their winters

Timeline of Sacagawea's Life

sometime between 1798 and 1801
goes to live with the Hidatsa tribe

1788, 1789, or 1790
born (exact date unknown)

No one is sure how long Sacagawea lived after the trip. One thing is certain, though. It is hard to imagine the expedition without her. She was an interpreter, guide, cook, peacemaker, and more. She is one of America's earliest heroes.

1805
sets out with Corps of Discovery

1806
returns home
with her family

2000
the Sacagawea
dollar is introduced

A Poem About Sacagawea

Sacagawea hit the trail—
the only explorer who was not male!
Despite danger, hunger, snow, and hail,
with her as guide, the trip could not fail.

You Can Be an Explorer

- Do not be afraid of a challenge.
- Be on the lookout for new things to try.
- Be curious and open to adventure!

Glossary

expedition (ek-spuh-DI-shun): journey made for a specific reason

explorers (ek-SPLOR-uhrs): people who travel to discover what a place is like

interpreted (in-TUR-prit-ed): translated words from one language to another

route (ROOT): a way to travel from one place to another

Index

Facts for Now

Visit this Scholastic Web site for more information on Sacagawea:
www.factsfornow.scholastic.com
Enter the keyword **Sacagawea**

About the Author

Jodie Shepherd, who also writes under the name Leslie Kimmelman, is an award-winning author of dozens of books for children, both fiction and nonfiction. She is a children's book editor, too.